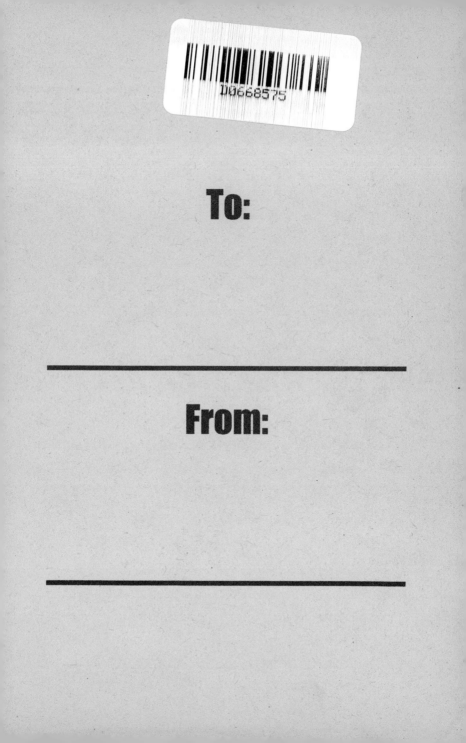

To:

_____

From:

_____

My Book of Devotions

A Guide for Parents & Kids

about Obedience

Simon & Schuster, Inc.

NEW YORK LONDON TORONTO SYDNEY

Simon & Schuster, Inc.

1230 Avenue of the Americas, New York, New York 10020

Cover Design by Kim Russell / Wahoo Designs
Page Layout by Bart Dawson

Manufactured in the United States of America

10 9 8 7 6 5 4 3 2

ISBN-13: 978-1-4169-1579-9
ISBN-10: 1-4169-1579-6

My Book of Devotions

A Guide for Parents & Kids

about Obedience

I will praise thee with
my whole heart . . . .

Psalm 138:1 KJV

Table of Contents

A Message to Parents   13

1. God Has Rules   15
2. Your Family Has Rules   19
3. It's in the Bible   23
4. Self-control   27
5. Obeying Your Parents   31
6. Think About It First   35
7. Obedience Is a Choice   39
8. Choosing the Right Words   43
9. Sharing the Love   47
10. The Golden Rule   51
11. Choices Have Consequences   55
12. Honesty Is the Best Policy   59
13. Don't Whine!   63
14. Going Along with the Crowd?   67
15. When You Don't Get Your Way
      (Tantrums Are Not Us)   71
16. Obey and Be Happy   75
17. Pray About It!   79
18. If You're Not Sure What's Right,
      Ask Somebody!   83

19. Respecting Authority   87
20. Learning How to Be Wise   91
21. Obey Your Teachers   95
22. Good Deeds Are a Good Thing   99
23. Going to Church   103
24. What Kind of Example?   107
25. Obey and Be Joyful   111
26. Choosing Your Friends   115
27. Saying What's Right   119
28. Jesus Is Our Example   123
29. Patience Pays   127
30. Showing How We Love God   131
31. For God So Loved the World   135

Bible Verses to Remember   139

A Message to Parents

Perhaps your child's bookshelf is already filled with a happy and helpful assortment of good books for kids. If so, congratulations—that means you're a thoughtful parent who understands the importance of reading to your child. This book is intended to be an important addition to your child's library.

This little text is intended to be read by Christian parents to their young children. The book contains 31 brief chapters, one for each day of the month. Each chapter consists of a Bible verse, a brief story, kid-friendly quotations from notable Christian thinkers, a timely tip, and a prayer. Every chapter examines a different aspect of an important topic: obedience.

For the next 31 days, take the time to read one chapter each night to your child, and then spend a few moments talking about the chapter's meaning. By the end of the month, you will have had 31 different opportunities to share God's wisdom with your son or daughter, and that's good . . . very good.

If you have been touched by God's love and His grace, then you know the joy that He has brought into your own life. Now it's your turn to share His message with the boy or girl whom He has entrusted to your care. Happy reading! And may God richly bless you and yours.

God Has Rules

We can be sure that we know God
if we obey his commands.
1 John 2:3 NCV

Day 1

God has rules, and He wants you to obey them. He wants you to be fair, honest, and kind. He wants you to behave yourself, and He wants you to respect your parents. God has other rules, too, and you'll find them in a very special book: the Bible.

With a little help from your parents, you can figure out God's rules. And then, it's up to you to live by them. When you do, everybody will be pleased—you'll be pleased, your parents will be pleased . . . and God will be pleased, too.

Big Idea for Kids

Obeying God? Yes! What about all those rules you learn about in the Bible? Well, those aren't just any old rules—they're God's rules. And you should behave—and obey—accordingly.

Nobody is good by accident.
C. H. Spurgeon

Big Idea for Parents

Teaching Them Obedience: Your children will learn about life from many sources; the most important source should be you. But remember that the lectures you give are never as important as the ones you live.

Today's Prayer

Dear Lord, I trust you, and I know
that Your rules are good for me.
I will do my best to obey You,
even when it's hard.
Amen

Your Family Has Rules

You must choose for yourselves today
whom you will serve . . .
as for me and my family,
we will serve the Lord.
Joshua 24:15 NCV

Day 2

Face facts: your family has rules . . . rules that you're not supposed to break.

If you're old enough to know right from wrong, then you're old enough to do something about it. In other words, you should always try to obey your family's rules.

How can you tell "the right thing" from "the wrong thing"? By listening carefully to your parents, that's how.

The more self-control you have, the easier it is to obey your parents. Why? Because when you learn to think first and do things next, you avoid making silly mistakes. So here's what you should do: First, slow down long enough to listen to your parents. Then, do the things that you know your parents want you to do.

Face facts: your family has rules . . . and it's better for everybody when you obey them.

Big Idea for Kids

Since you love your family . . . show it by behaving yourself and obeying your family's rules!

> The child that never learns to obey
> his parents in the home will not
> obey God or man out of the home.
> Susanna Wesley

Big Idea for Parents

Wise parents know what to overlook. Expect your child to be well-behaved, but don't expect your child to be perfect.

Today's Prayer

Dear Lord, You have given me a family
that cares for me and loves me.
Thank You. Let me love everybody
in my family, even when they're not
perfect. And let me always be thankful
that my family loves me even when
I'm not perfect.
Amen

It's in the Bible

Your word is like a lamp for my feet
and a light for my way.
Psalm 119:105 ICB

What book contains everything that God has to say about obedience? The Bible, of course. If you read the Bible every day, you'll soon be convinced that obedience is very important to God. And, since obedience is important to God, it should be important to you, too.

The Bible is the most important book you'll ever own. It's God's Holy Word. Read it every day, and follow its instructions. If you do, you'll be a more obedient person . . . and you'll be safe now and forever.

Big Idea for Kids

Do you take care of your Bible? Hopefully so! After all, it's the most important book you'll ever own!

> The Bible is the treasure map that leads us to God's highest treasures.
> Max Lucado

Big Idea for Parents

How can you teach your children the importance of God's Holy Word? By example. When teaching your child about the Bible, words are fine—but actually studying the Bible is far better.

Today's Prayer

Dear Lord, the Bible is Your gift to me.
Let me use it, let me trust it,
and let me obey it,
today and every day.
Amen

Self-control

Knowing God leads to self-control.
Self-control leads to patient endurance,
and patient endurance leads to godliness.
2 Peter 1:6 NLT

Learning how to control yourself helps you become a more obedient person. So the more you learn about self-control, the better.

Learning how to control yourself is a good thing. Self-control helps you at home, at school, and at church. That's why parents and teachers are happy to talk about the rewards of good behavior.

If you want to learn more about self-control, ask your parents. They'll help you figure out better ways to behave yourself. And that's good for everybody . . . especially you!

Big Idea for Kids

A big part of growing up . . . is learning how to control yourself.

Your thoughts are the determining factor
as to whose mold you are conformed to.
Control your thoughts and you control
the direction of your life.
Charles Stanley

Big Idea for Parents

Self-control at school starts at home: teachers can certainly help, but we cannot expect them to re-train our children. When it comes to the importance of self-control, we, as parents, must be the ones to teach our kids how to behave.

Today's Prayer

Dear Lord, I want to be able to control myself better and better each day. Help me find better ways to behave myself in ways that are pleasing to You.
Amen

Obeying Your Parents

Children, obey your parents in all things:
for this is well-pleasing unto the Lord.
Colossians 3:20 KJV

Day 5

When your parents ask you to do something, do you usually obey them or do you usually ignore them? When your parents try to get your attention, do you listen or not? When your parents make rules, do you obey those rules or do you break them? Hopefully, you've learned to listen to your parents and to obey.

In order to be an obedient person, you must first learn how to control yourself—otherwise, you won't be able to behave yourself even if you want to. Controlling yourself means that you must slow down long enough to listen to your parents, and then you must be willing to do something about the things your parents tell you to do.

When you learn the importance of being obedient, you'll soon discover that good things happen when you behave yourself. And the sooner you learn to listen and to obey, the sooner those good things will start happening to you!

Big Idea for Kids

When you obey your parents . . . you're pleasing God, you're pleasing your parents, and you're doing yourself a BIG favor.

He intended families to be the safe haven
where children are born and raised,
a place where the tender shoots are
nurtured until their roots grow
strong and deep.
Carol Kuykendall

Big Idea for Parents

Have a Few Important Rules . . . and enforce them.

Today's Prayer

Dear Lord, when I obey Your rules,
good things happen. One of Your rules
is pretty simple: to obey my parents.
So here's what I'm asking for, Lord:
Help me listen to my parents . . .
and help me obey them.
Amen

Think About It First

So prepare your minds for service and
have self-control. All your hope should be
for the gift of grace that will be yours
when Jesus Christ is shown to you.

1 Peter 1:13 NCV

Day 6

Maybe you've heard this old saying: "Look before you leap." What does that saying mean? It means that you should stop and think before you do something. Otherwise, you might be sorry you did it.

Learning how to control yourself is an important part of growing up. The more you learn about self-control, the better. Self-control will help you at home, at school, and at church. That's why parents and teachers are happy to talk about the rewards of good self-control. And that's why you should be excited about learning how important it is to look before you leap . . . not after!

Big Idea for Kids

Controlling yourself by slowing yourself down: Sometimes, the best way to control yourself is to slow yourself down. Then, you can think about the things you're about to do before you do them.

> Plan ahead—it wasn't raining
> when Noah built the ark.
> Anonymous

Big Idea for Parents

Be patient with your child's impatience: children are supposed to be more impulsive than adults; after all, they're still kids. So be understanding of your child's limitations and understanding of his or her imperfections.

Today's Prayer

Dear Lord, the Bible teaches me that it's good to be able to control myself. Today, I will slow myself down and think about things before I do things. Amen

Obedience Is a Choice

Do what God's teaching says;
when you only listen and do nothing,
you are fooling yourselves.
James 1:22 NCV

You have a choice to make: are you going to be an obedient person or not? And remember: the decision to be obedient—or the decision not to be obedient—is a decision that you must make for yourself.

If you decide to behave yourself, you've made a smart choice. If you decide to obey your parents, you've made another smart choice. If you decide to pay attention to your teachers, you've made yet another wise choice. BUT . . . if you decide not to be obedient, you've made a silly choice.

What kind of person will you choose to be? An obedient, well-behaved person . . . or the opposite? Before you answer that question, here's something to think about: obedience pays . . . and disobedience doesn't.

Big Idea for Kids

When you make wise choices . . . You make everybody happy. You make your parents happy, you make your teachers happy, you make your friends happy, and you make God happy!

Life is pretty much like a cafeteria line—
it offers us many choices,
both good and bad. Choose wisely.
Dennis Swanberg

Big Idea for Parents

Some things are not debatable: Some matters should be strictly up to you, the parent. These kinds of choices include issues of personal health and safety and the core principles by which you, as a concerned mom or dad, intend to raise your family.

Today's Prayer

Dear Lord, help me make choices that please You. Help me to be honest, patient, and kind. And above all, help me to follow the teachings of Jesus, not just today, but every day.

Amen

Choosing the Right Words

Don't use foul or abusive language.
Let everything you say be good and helpful,
so that your words will be an encouragement
to those who hear them.
Ephesians 4:29 NLT

Your words can help people . . . or not. Make certain that you're the kind of person who says helpful things, not hurtful things. You'll feel better about yourself when you help other people feel better about themselves.

Do you like for people to say kind words to you? Of course you do! And that's exactly how other people feel, too. That's why it's so important to say things that make people feel better, not worse.

Everybody needs to hear kind words, and that's exactly the kind of words they should hear from you!

Big Idea for Kids

Think before you speak: If you want to keep from hurting other people's feelings, don't open your mouth until you've turned on your brain.

When you talk, choose the very same words that you would use if Jesus were looking over your shoulder. Because He is.

Marie T. Freeman

Big Idea for Parents

Parents set the boundaries: Whether they realize it or not, parents (not kids) establish the general tone of the conversations that occur within their homes. And it's up to parents to ensure that the tone of those conversations is a tone that's pleasing to God.

Today's Prayer

Dear Lord, I will try to show respect
to everybody, starting with my family
and my friends. And, I will do
my best to share the love that
I feel in my heart for them . . .
and for You!
Amen

Sharing the Love

Jesus answered, "'Love the Lord your God with all your heart, all your soul, and all your mind.' This is the first and most important command. And the second command is like the first: 'Love your neighbor as you love yourself.' All the law and the writings of the prophets depend on these two commands."

Matthew 22:37-40 NCV

Day 9

The Bible teaches us that God is love and that if we wish to know Him, we must have love in our hearts. Sometimes, of course, when we're tired, angry, or frustrated, it is very hard for us to be loving. Thankfully, anger and frustration are feelings that come and go, but God's love lasts forever.

If you'd like to improve your day and your life, share God's love with your family and friends. Every time you love, and every time you give, God smiles.

Big Idea for Kids

Express yourself . . . Since you love your family, you should tell them so . . . a lot!

The secret of a happy home life is that the members of the family learn to give and receive love.

Billy Graham

Big Idea for Parents

Be Expressive: Make certain that at your house love is expressed and demonstrated many times each day. Little acts of consideration and kindness can make a big difference in the way that your child feels and the way your child behaves.

Today's Prayer

Dear Lord, today and every day,
I will tell my family that I love them.
And I will show my family
that I love them, too.
Amen

The Golden Rule

Do for other people the same things
you want them to do for you.
Matthew 7:12 ICB

Day 10

How should you treat other people? Jesus has the answer to that question. Jesus wants you to treat other people exactly like you want to be treated: with kindness, respect, and courtesy. When you do, you'll make your family and friends happy . . . and that's what God wants.

So if you're wondering how to treat someone else, follow the Golden Rule: treat the other people like you want them to treat you. When you do, you'll be obeying your Father in heaven, and you'll be making other folks happy at the same time.

Big Idea for Kids

How would you feel? When you're trying to decide how to treat another person, ask yourself this question: "How would I feel if somebody treated me that way?" Then, treat the other person the way that you would want to be treated.

> The Golden Rule starts at home,
> but it should never stop there.
> Marie T. Freeman

Big Idea for Parents

The Golden Rule . . . is as good as gold—in fact, it's better than gold. And as a responsible parent, you should make certain that your child knows that the Golden Rule is, indeed, golden.

Today's Prayer

Dear God, help me remember to treat
other people in the same way that
I would want to be treated if I were
in their shoes. The Golden Rule is
Your rule, Father; I'll make it
my rule, too.
Amen

Choices Have Consequences

Do not be fooled: You cannot cheat God.
People harvest only what they plant.
Galatians 6:7-8 NCV

Day 11

There's really no way to get around it: choices matter. If you make good choices, good things will usually happen to you. And if you make bad choices, bad things will usually happen.

The next time you have an important choice to make, ask yourself this: "Am I doing what God wants me to do?" If you can answer that question with a great big "YES," then go ahead. But if you're not sure if the choice you are about to make is right, slow down. Why? Because choices matter . . . a lot!

Big Idea for Kids

Think ahead: Before you do something, ask yourself this question: "Will I be ashamed if my parents find out?" If the answer to that question is "Yes," don't do it!

It is easy to dodge our responsibilities, but we cannot dodge the consequences of dodging our responsibilities.
Josiah Stamp

Big Idea for Parents

Logical Consequences! The world won't protect your child from the consequences of misbehavior, and neither should you. As a parent, your job is to ensure that the consequences of your child's actions are logical, measured, appropriate, and thoroughly understood by your youngster.

Today's Prayer

Dear Lord, when I play by Your rules,
You bless my life. But, when I disobey
Your rules, I suffer the consequences.
Help me obey You and my parents . . .
starting right now!
Amen

Honesty
Is the Best Policy

Doing what is right brings freedom
to honest people.
Proverbs 11:6 ICB

Day 12

Have you ever said something that wasn't true? When you did, were you sorry for what you had said? Probably so.

When we're dishonest, we make ourselves unhappy in surprising ways. Here are just a few troubles that result from dishonesty: we feel guilty and we are usually found out and we disappoint others and we disappoint God. It's easy to see that lies always cause more problems than they solve.

Happiness and honesty always go hand in hand. But it's up to you to make sure that you go hand in hand with them!

Big Idea for Kids

When telling the truth is hard . . . it probably means that you're afraid of what others might think—or what they might do—if you're truthful. But even when telling the truth is hard, it's always the right thing to do.

> I hold the maxim no less applicable
> to public than to private affairs,
> that honesty is the best policy.
>
> George Washington

Big Idea for Parents

The truth can be hard for parents, too: telling the truth isn't just hard for kids. And when honesty is hard, that's precisely the moment when wise parents remember that their children are watching . . . and learning.

Today's Prayer

Dear Lord, sometimes it's hard to tell
the truth. But even when telling
the truth is difficult, let me follow
Your commandment. Honesty isn't just
the best policy, Lord; it's Your policy,
and I will obey You by making it
my policy, too.
Amen

Don't Whine!

Your attitude should be the same
that Christ Jesus had.
Philippians 2:5 NLT

Day 13

Do you like to listen to other children whine? No way! And since you don't like to hear other kids whining, then you certainly shouldn't whine either.

Sometimes, kids think that whining is a good way to get the things they want . . . but it's not! So if your parents or your teacher asks you to do something, don't complain about it. And if there's something you want, don't whine and complain until you get it.

Remember: whining won't make you happy . . . and it won't make anybody else happy either.

Big Idea for Kids

Two special words: Thank you! Your parents and your teachers will never become tired of hearing those two little words. Say them often.

> Shine—don't whine.
> Anonymous

Big Idea for Parents

Count your blessings . . . and keep counting. Whining can be contagious, so make sure that your home is, to the greatest extent possible, a whine-free zone. How can you do this? A good way to start is by counting your blessings, not your problems.

Today's Prayer

Dear Lord, I'm really thankful for
all the good things I have.
Today I will show You how grateful
I am, not only by the words that
I speak, but also by the way that I act.
Amen

Going Along with the Crowd?

Obviously, I'm not trying to be
a people pleaser!
No, I am trying to please God.

Galatians 1:10 NLT

Day 14

If you're like most people, you have probably been tempted to "go along with the crowd" . . . even when the crowd was misbehaving. But here's something to think about: just because your friends may be misbehaving doesn't mean that you have to misbehave, too.

When people behave badly, they can spoil things in a hurry. So make sure that they don't spoil things for you.

So, if your friends misbehave, don't copy them! Instead, do the right thing. You'll be glad you did . . . and so will God!

Big Idea for Kids

You simply cannot please everybody. So here's what you should do: Try pleasing God and your parents.

> You should forget about trying to be
> popular with everybody and start
> trying to be popular with God Almighty.
> Sam Jones

Big Idea for Parents

Old-fashioned respect never goes out of fashion: Remember the good old days when parents demanded that their children be polite and respectful, especially to adults? For wise parents, those good old days are now.

Today's Prayer

Dear Lord, today I will honor You with my thoughts, my actions, and my prayers. I will try to please You, and I will try to serve You.
Amen

When You Don't Get Your Way (Tantrums Are Not Us)

A foolish person loses his temper.
But a wise person controls his anger.
Proverbs 29:11 ICB

Day 15

Temper tantrums are so silly. And so is pouting. So, of course, is whining. When we lose our tempers, we say things that we shouldn't say, and we do things that we shouldn't do. Too bad!

The Bible tells us that it is foolish to become angry and that it is wise to remain calm. That's why we should learn to control our tempers before our tempers control us.

Big Idea for Kids

No more temper tantrums! If you think you're about to throw a tantrum, slow down, catch your breath, and walk away if you must. It's better to walk away than it is to strike out in anger.

> Anger is a kind of temporary madness.
> St. Basil the Great

Big Idea for Parents

Wise role models are a good thing to have: If you can control your anger, you'll help your children see the wisdom in controlling theirs.

Today's Prayer

Dear Lord, help me to keep away
from angry thoughts and angry people.
And if I am tempted to have
a temper tantrum, help me
to calm down before I do.
Amen

Obey and Be Happy

But the truly happy person is the one
who carefully studies God's perfect law
that makes people free. He continues to
study it. He listens to God's teaching
and does not forget what he heard.
Then he obeys what God's teaching says.
When he does this, it makes him happy.

James 1:25 ICB

Day 16

Do you want to be happy? Then you should learn to obey your parents and your teachers. And, of course, you should also learn to obey God. When you do, you'll discover that happiness goes hand-in-hand with good behavior.

The happiest people do not misbehave; the happiest people are not cruel or greedy. The happiest people don't disobey their parents, their teachers, or their Father in heaven. The happiest people are those who obey the rules.

And it's up to you to make sure that you're one of those happy people.

Big Idea for Kids

Good behavior leads to a happy life. And bad behavior doesn't.

Happiness is obedience,
and obedience is happiness.
C. H. Spurgeon

Big Idea for Parents

Your positive responses to their positive behavior: When your child does something good, applaud loudly. When you do, you'll make two people happy.

Today's Prayer

Dear Heavenly Father, when I obey,
I'm a much happier person.
Help me learn the importance of
obeying my parents and
the importance of obeying You.
Amen

Pray About It!

Always be happy. Never stop praying.
Give thanks whatever happens.
That is what God wants for you
in Christ Jesus.
1 Thessalonians: 5:16-18 ICB

Day 17

Do you really want to become a more obedient person? Then pray about it. Would you like to learn how to behave yourself a little bit better? Then pray about it.

If you have questions about whether you should do something or not, pray about it. If there is something you're worried about, ask God to comfort you. And as you pray more, you'll discover that God is always near and that He's always ready to hear from you. So don't worry about things; pray about them. God is waiting . . . and listening!

Big Idea for Kids

Eyelids closed... or not! When you are praying, the position of your eyelids is makes little or no difference. Of course it's good to close your eyes and bow your head whenever you can, but it's also good to offer quick prayers to God with your eyes—and your heart—wide.

> Prayer accomplishes more
> than anything else.
> Bill Bright

Big Idea for Parents

Don't ever be embarrassed to pray: Are you embarrassed to bow your head in a restaurant? Don't be; it's the people who aren't praying who should be embarrassed!

Today's Prayer

Dear Lord, help me remember
the importance of prayer.
You always hear my prayers, God;
let me always pray them!
Amen

If You're Not Sure What's Right, Ask Somebody!

Continue to ask, and God will give to you.
Continue to search, and you will find.
Continue to knock, and the door
will open for you.

Matthew 7:7 ICB

Day 18

When you're not sure about something, are you willing to ask your parents what you should do? Hopefully, when you have a question, you're not afraid to ask.

If you've got lots of questions, the Bible promises that God—like your parents—has answers, too.

So don't ever be afraid to ask questions. Both your parents and your Heavenly Father want to hear your questions . . . and they want to answer your questions as soon as you ask.

Big Idea for Kids

Pray about it: Whatever it is, God can handle it. So ask Him to help you . . . and while you're at it, ask your parents for help, too.

God guides through the counsel
of good people.
E. Stanley Jones

Big Idea for Parents

Parents should ask for help, too. If you need something, ask. And remember this: God is listening, and He wants to hear from you right now.

Today's Prayer

Dear Lord, the Bible tells me
that when I ask for Your help,
You will give it. I thank You, Lord,
for Your help, for Your love,
and for Your Son.
Amen

Respecting Authority

Show respect for all people.
Love the brothers and sisters
of God's family.
1 Peter 2:17 ICB

*A*re you polite and respectful to your parents and teachers? And do you do your best to treat everybody with the respect they deserve? If you want to obey God's rules, then you should be able to answer yes to these questions.

Remember this: the Bible teaches you to be a respectful person—and if it's right there in the Bible, it's certainly the right thing to do!

Big Idea for Kids

Everybody is a VIP: VIP means "Very Important Person." To God, everybody is a VIP, and we should treat every person with dignity, patience, and respect.

It is my calling to treat every human being
with grace and dignity, to treat every
person, whether encountered in a palace
or a gas station, as a life made
in the image of God.
Sheila Walsh

Big Idea for Parents

Respect for authority starts with you. Remember this: respect for those in authority begins at the head of the household and works its way down from there. And remember one more thing: your kids are watching every move you make!

Today's Prayer

Dear God, I pray for those who care for me, especially my parents. Give them wisdom, courage, compassion, and faith.

Amen

Learning How
to Be Wise

Wisdom is a tree of life to those
who eat her fruit; happy is the man
who keeps on eating it.
Proverbs 3:18 TLB

Day 20

If you look in a dictionary, you'll see that the word "wisdom" means "using good judgement, and knowing what is true." But there's more: it's not enough just to know what's right; if you really want to become a wise person, you must also do what's right.

A big part of "doing what's right" is learning to be obedient . . . and the best time to start being a more obedient person is right now! Why? Because it's the wise thing to do.

Big Idea for Kids

When you are wrong admit it. God will be happy and so will your parents.

> Wisdom is the power to put our time
> and our knowledge to proper use.
> Thomas J. Watson

Big Idea for Parents

Parents make mistakes, too. When you are wrong, admit it. When you do, your children will learn that it's far better to fix problems than to ignore them.

Today's Prayer

Dear Lord, there's a right way to do things and a wrong way to do things. When I do things that are wrong, help me be quick to ask for forgiveness . . . and quick to correct my mistakes. Amen

Obey Your Teachers

From a wise mind comes wise speech;
the words of the wise are persuasive.
Proverbs 16:23 NLT

Day 21

It's good to obey your teachers, but before you can obey them, you must make sure you understand what your teachers are saying. So, in order to be an obedient student, you must be a student who knows how to listen.

Once you decide to be a careful listener, you'll become a better learner, too. But if you're determined to talk to other kids while your teachers are teaching, you won't learn very much.

So do yourself a favor: when you go to school, listen and obey. You'll be glad you did . . . and your teachers will be glad, too.

Big Idea for Kids

Learning how to obey makes you a better person. You have many teachers. Listen to them and obey them. When you do, you'll become a better person.

Obedience is the key of knowledge.
Christina Rossetti

Big Idea for Parents

Teaching the importance of teachers: You understand that your child's teachers are "Very Important People." Make certain that your child understands it, too.

Today's Prayer

Dear Lord, thank You for giving me so many wise teachers. Help me listen carefully to my teachers, and help me learn from them.

Amen

Good Deeds Are a Good Thing

A good person produces good deeds
from a good heart.
Luke 6:45 NLT

It's good to do good deeds. Even when nobody's watching, God is. And God knows whether you've done the right thing or the wrong thing.

So if you're tempted to misbehave when nobody is looking, remember this: There is never a time when "nobody's watching." Somebody is always watching over you—and that Somebody, of course, is your Father in Heaven. Don't let Him down!

Big Idea for Kids

You must do more than talk about it: In order to be a good person, you must do good things. So get busy! The best time to do a good deed is as soon as you can do it!

> Seek to do good, and you will find that happiness will run after you.
> James Freeman Clarke

Big Idea for Parents

Parental love in action . . . Of course, it's good to tell your kids how you feel about them, but that's not enough. You should also show your children how you feel with your good deeds and your kind words.

Today's Prayer

Dear Lord, let me help others in every
way that I can. Jesus served others;
I can too. I will serve other people
with my good deeds and with my
prayers, and I will give thanks for
all those who serve and protect
our nation and our world.

Amen

Going to Church

Let's see how inventive we can be in
encouraging love and helping out,
not avoiding worshipping together
as some do but spurring each other on.
Hebrews 10:24-25 MSG

When your parents take you to church, are you pleased to go? Hopefully so. After all, church is a wonderful place to learn about God's rules.

The church belongs to God just as surely as you belong to God. That's why the church is a good place to learn about God and about His Son Jesus.

So when your mom and dad take you to church, remember this: church is a fine place to be . . . and you're lucky to be there.

Big Idea for Kids

Forget the Excuses: If somebody starts making up reasons not to go to church, don't pay any attention . . . even if that person is you!

The church is where it's at.
The first place of Christian service
for any Christian is in a local church.
Jerry Clower

Big Idea for Parents

Make church a celebration, not an obligation: Your attitude towards church will help determine your kids' attitude toward church . . . so celebrate accordingly!

Today's Prayer

Dear Lord, thank You for Your church.
I'll go to church and support it.
I'll help build Your church, Lord,
in every way I can.
Amen

What Kind of Example?

You are the light that gives light to the world...Live so that they will see the good things you do. Live so that they will praise your Father in heaven.

Matthew 5:14,16 ICB

Day 24

What kind of example are you? Are you the kind of person who shows other people what it means to be obedient and kind? Hopefully so!!!

Are you willing to obey your parents? And are you willing to obey God? If so, then you're bound to be a good example to other people. And that's a good thing because God needs people like you who are willing to stand up and be counted for Him.

Big Idea for Kids

Let your light shine . . . The way that you behave yourself is like a light that shines out upon the world. Make sure that your light is both bright and good.

More depends on my walk than my talk.
D. L. Moody

Big Idea for Parents

Words are never enough: When it comes to teaching our children the most important lessons, the things we say pale in comparison to the things we do. Being a responsible parent is a big job, but don't fret: you and God, working together, can handle it!

Today's Prayer

Dear Lord, make me a good example to
my family and friends. Let the things
that I say and do show everybody what
it means to be a good person
and a good Christian.
Amen

Obey and Be Joyful

Light shines on the godly, and joy on those who do right. May all who are godly be happy in the Lord and praise his holy name.

Psalm 97:11-12 NLT

Day 25

A man named C. S. Lewis once said, "Joy is the serious business of heaven." And he was right! God seriously wants you to be a seriously joyful person.

One way that you can have a more joyful life is by learning how to become a more obedient person. When you do, you'll stay out of trouble, and you'll have lots more time for fun.

So here's a way to be a more joyful, happy person: do the right thing! It's the best way to live.

Big Idea for Kids

Joy doesn't come from having things . . . Joy comes from doing the right thing.

Joy is the echo of God's life within us.
Joseph Marmion

Big Idea for Parents

Joy is contagious: Remember that a joyful family starts with joyful parents.

Today's Prayer

Dear Lord, I want to be a joyful
Christian, and I know that my joy
depends, in part, on my obedience.
Today, I will try to be both
obedient and joyful.
Amen

Choosing Your Friends

A friend loves you all the time.
Proverbs 17:17 ICB

Day 26

Are your friends the kind of kids who encourage you to behave yourself? If so, you've chosen your friends wisely.

But if your friends try to get you in trouble, perhaps it's time to think long and hard about making some new friends.

Whether you know it or not, you're probably going to behave like your friends behave. So pick out friends who make you want to behave better, not worse. When you do, you'll be saving yourself from a lot of trouble . . . a whole lot of trouble.

Big Idea for Kids

You make friends by being a friend. And when you choose your friends, choose wisely.

Do you want to be wise?
Choose wise friends.

Charles Swindoll

Big Idea for Parents

Help from the sidelines: As parents, we can't make friendships for our children, but we can coach them on the art of making friends. All of us, whether youngsters or grown-ups, make friends by treating others as we wish to be treated.

Today's Prayer

Thank You Lord, for the Friend
I have in Jesus. And, thank You for
all my other friends, too.
Amen

Saying What's Right

Speak the truth to each other . . . .
Zechariah 8:16 NIV

Day 27

Sometimes, it's hard to know exactly what to say. And sometimes it can be very tempting to say something that isn't true—or something that isn't nice. But when you say things you shouldn't say, you'll regret it later.

So make this promise to yourself, and keep it—promise to think about the things you say before you say them. And whatever you do, always tell the truth. When you do these things, you'll be doing yourself a big favor, and you'll be obeying the Word of God.

Big Idea for Kids

If you're not sure that it's the right thing to say, don't say it! And if you're not sure that it's the truth, don't tell it.

Those who walk in truth walk in liberty.

Beth Moore

Big Idea for Parents

Words, words, words . . . are important, important, important! And, some of the most important words you will ever speak are the ones that your children hear. So whether or not you are talking directly to your kids, choose your words carefully.

Today's Prayer

Dear Lord, when I'm about to
say something, help me think about
my words before I say them, not after.
Amen

Jesus Is Our Example

I have set you an example that
you should do as I have done for you.
John 13:15 NIV

How do people know that you're a Christian? Well, you can tell them, of course. And make no mistake about it: talking about your faith in God is a very good thing to do. But telling people about Jesus isn't enough. You should also show people how a Christian (like you) should behave.

God wants you to be loving and giving. That way, when another other person sees how you behave, that person will know what it means to be a good Christian . . . a good Christian like you!

Big Idea for Kids

If You Want to be a little more like Christ
. . . learn about His teachings, follow in His
footsteps, and obey His commandments.

> In his life, Christ is an example
> showing us how to live.
> Martin Luther

Big Idea for Parents

Kids imitate their parents, so act accordingly!
The best way for your children to learn how
to follow in Christ's footsteps is by following
you while you follow Him!

Today's Prayer

Dear Lord, You sent Jesus to save the world and to save me. I thank You for Jesus, and I will do my best to follow Him, today and forever.
Amen

Patience Pays

Always be humble and gentle.
Be patient and accept each other with love.
Ephesians 4:2 ICB

Day 29

The dictionary defines the word "patience" as "the ability to be calm, tolerant, and understanding." Here's what that means: the word "calm" means being in control of your emotions (not letting your emotions control you). The word "tolerant" means being kind and considerate to people who are different from you. And, the word "understanding" means being able to put yourself in another person's shoes.

If you can be calm, tolerant, and understanding, you will be the kind of person whose good deeds are a blessing to your family and friends. And that's exactly the kind of person that God wants you to be.

Big Idea for Kids

Be patient, and follow the rules . . . even if you don't like some of the rules that you're supposed to follow, follow them anyway.

If only we could be as patient with
other people as God is with us!
Jim Gallery

Big Idea for Parents

Kids imitate their parents, so act accordingly! The best way for your child to learn to be patient is by example . . . your example!

Today's Prayer

Lord, sometimes it's hard to be a patient person, and that's exactly when I should try my hardest to be patient. Help me to obey Your commandments by being a patient, loving Christian, even when it's hard. Amen

Showing How
We Love God

This is love for God: to obey his commands.
1 John 5:3 NIV

Day 30

How can you show God how much you love Him? By obeying His commandments, that's how! When you follow God's rules, you show Him that you have real respect for Him and for His Son.

Sometimes, you will be tempted to disobey God, but don't do it. And sometimes you'll be tempted to disobey your parents or your teachers . . . but don't do that, either.

When your parent steps away or a teacher looks away, it's up to you to control yourself. And of this you can be sure: If you really want to control yourself, you can do it!

Big Idea for Kids

When should you get tired of obeying God? The answer to that question is simple: Never!

> God's mark is on everything
> that obeys Him.
> Martin Luther

Big Idea for Parents

Calling all parents! What the world needs is more parents who are willing to be positive role models to their children. God wants you to be that kind of parent . . . now!

Today's Prayer

Lord, let Your will be my will.
Let me always seek Your guidance
and Your will for my life.
Amen

For God So Loved the World

For God loved the world in this way:
He gave His only Son, so that everyone
who believes in Him will not perish
but have eternal life.
John 3:16 Holman CSB

Day 31

How much does God love you? He loves you so much that He sent His Son Jesus to come to this earth for you! And, when you accept Jesus into your heart, God gives you a gift that is more precious than gold: that gift is called "eternal life," which means that you will live forever with God in heaven!

God's love is bigger and more powerful than anybody can imagine, but it is very real. So do yourself a favor right now: accept God's love with open arms and welcome His Son Jesus into your heart. When you do, your life will be changed today, tomorrow, and forever.

Big Idea for Kids

God's love is your greatest security blanket. Think how much your parents love you and then know that God loves your even more.

The greatest love of all is God's love for us, a love that showed itself in action.
Billy Graham

Big Idea for Parents

The kids are watching . . . Children form their ideas about God's love by experiencing their parents' love. Live—and love— accordingly.

Today's Prayer

Dear God, the Bible teaches me that
Your love lasts forever. Thank You,
God, for Your love. Let me trust
Your promises, and let me live
according to Your teachings,
not just for today, but forever.
Amen

Bible Verses
to Remember

Be an example to show the believers how they should live.

1 Timothy 4:12 ICB

Good people are rewarded . . . evil people are paid back with punishment.

Proverbs 10:16 ICB

Be still, and know that I am God . . . .

Psalm 46:10 KJV

My child, listen to your father's teaching. And do not forget your mother's advice.

Proverbs 1:8 ICB

Be kind to each other, tenderhearted,
forgiving one another, just as God
through Christ has forgiven you.

Ephesians 4:32 NLT

Yes, if you forgive others for
the things they do wrong,
then your Father in heaven will also
forgive you for the things
you do wrong.

Matthew 6:14 ICB

I say this because I know what
I am planning for you," says the Lord.
"I have good plans for you, not plans
to hurt you. I will give you hope
and a good future."

Jeremiah 29:11 NCV

Likewise you younger people, submit yourselves to your elders.

1 Peter 5:5 NKJV

Make the most of every opportunity.

Colossians 4:5 NIV

For God has not given us
a spirit of fear,
but of power and of love
and of a sound mind.

2 Timothy 1:7 NLT

I can do everything
through him
that gives me strength.

Philippians 4:13 NIV

A new commandment I give to you,
that you love one another;
as I have loved you,
that you also love one another.

John 13:34 NKJV

I tell you the truth, whatever you did for one of the least of these brothers of mine, you did for me.

Matthew 25:40 NIV

Honor your father and your mother.

Exodus 20:12 ICB

Your word is a lamp for my feet and a light on my path.

Psalm 119:105 HCSB

Blessed are the peacemakers, for they will be called sons of God.

Matthew 5:9 NIV

We must not become tired of doing good.

Galatians 6:2 ICB